Dear Travel Professional,

Thanks for 'aspiring higher' –and pursuing higher levels of success and happiness! My sincere gratitude for your purchase. May the words in this unique book give lift to your business (and your life)!

What makes it unique? First, I've attempted to capture the rhythm and energy of a 'live' presentation for you. That's my style – to write what I speak. Second, I do some role-playing with you and transform from business coach to your client.

Life begins when we step into new comfort zones – and I hope I establish a prosperous new one for you. I know you'll soon jump for joy whenever a new lead arrives drops into your inbox!

Helping entrepreneurs to achieve higher levels of success and happiness is my passion. As I approach thirty years of dedication to our great travel industry, I remain the quintessential travel agent advocate. *It is my sincere wish that I inspire **you** to achieve greatly.*

In Your Pocket,

Stuart Lloyd Cohen

Chief Motivation Officer

www.StuartLloydCohen.com

Table of Contents

For even more outstanding resources and to find out how Stuart can present at your next big meeting please visit www.StuartLloydCohen.com

CHAPTER 1: Introduction

All TA's place CONTACT ME buttons online. The mission? To attract email leads and make new sales. Do you fish for new clients online? If you do, then you are encouraging browsers to ask for help. That said, let's be honest: when a new lead drops in the box, do you get excited or stressed?

Most TA's seem to get stressed and irritated. E-leads are widely viewed in many industries as time-wasting interruptions that rarely turn into sales.

Here's a twist: I believe the person sending the e-lead is actually more frustrated then you. Why on earth would a consumer complete a CONTACT ME form as a joke? Who has time for that?

I believe e-leads are terribly pre-judged and classified as junk mail unnecessarily. In turn, they get little respect and are treated poorly. What results is an unpleasant experience for two people: the TA and the person who sent the e-lead. Let's call that person "E."

Wait, did I just refer to E (the e-lead) as a person? Yes, I did. My mission today is to shock the TA into a new, healthier paradigm by introducing the person behind so-called junk mail.

So, get ready to meet E! I will take a back seat and let E do all the talking. You two can work this out. E just wants to book a vacation. You, TA, are getting in the way. Yet the TA believes E is getting in the way! (How's that for irony?)

Let me help you get out of each other's way and into each other's life. My mission is to help the TA turn e-leads into sales. My strategy is to get the TA to know E and to love E!

This is a "both-feet-IN" business proposition:

Get all in (or get all out).

If TA is tired of E's clogging the INBOX then opt-out now, please. Stop wasting the prospect's time (and giving TA's company a bad reputation). Let the lead go to the TA who truly wants it. When E receives poor treatment, the TA's company earns a bad rap. Plus, all TA's take a hit as an industry. I encourage TA's to decide to decide about E: love 'em or leave 'em!

CHAPTER 2:

Meet mE

I am E, your E-inquiry. I just landed in your INBOX. Are you happy to see mE? Or are you stressed to see mE drop in?

What is so bad about mE?

What is so good about mE?

I don't know you

You don't know mE

BUT you've got something I want,

And I've got something you want!

Why can't we all just get along?

Why on earth would you say CONTACT ME if you freak out every time an e-lead takes you up on your offer to help?

Either you want mE or you don't. Either put both feet in, or both feet out. I've got both feet in. I need a vacation. I expect you to have both feet in, too.

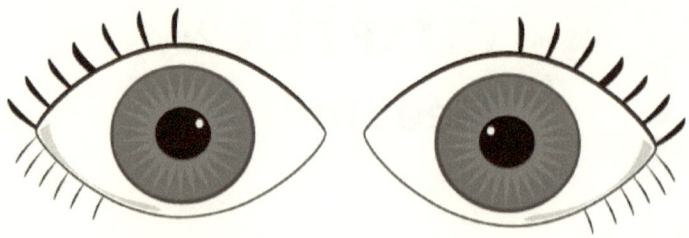

Success selling mE a vacation depends on how you see mE.

If you get stressed when I suddenly appear in your INBOX, then you regard mE as junk mail. I am an irritant. I am a time-waster, a day-spoiler. We won't get along very well if this is how you see mE.

Or you can see mE as an opportunity. **You can see mE as a real person**. I might become a really good client. Perhaps even a friend! What if I end up booking many trips with you, and I send my family to book with you, too? There is a chance you can make me very happy (and I can make you happy and a lot of money).

I am who you want mE to be. That's why I am here, speaking directly to you. If you get to know mE, maybe we can both achieve our mutual goals and get along just fine.

I am not comfortable booking online.

I did not click "book now," though I had hundreds of opportunities to do so. I did not (yet) book with another agent, though there are tens of thousands of choices.

I'm here, in your INBOX.

I'm there, in another agent's INBOX as well.

I'm at too much risk if I don't send out at least two CONTACT ME requests.

I'm up for grabs.

Whoever wants mE the most will get mE!

Today, I will tell you how.

CHAPTER 3:
What am I *really* feeling right now?

I am overwhelmed. There are so many choices! How do I choose the best vacation options? Get the best prices? Choose the best place to book? Booking a vacation is an overwhelming experience.

I am scared. I am scared to make wrong choices. My vacation time is limited and this is a big expense. I must choose right because I don't want to have any regrets. It's got to be right.

I need help. I cannot do it alone. Friends have given me tips. I have read a great deal online. I don't have a particular travel agent that I really like well enough to call for help. I am not comfortable making these choices and making this booking online or directly with a company.

Nobody loves mE. I have used the services of travel agents in the past but none were anything special. They booked me and then ignored me. I felt all they worried about was making the sale. Once I paid, they were done with me. I thought they loved me but I guess they did not. I honestly do not know if any travel agent can do better, so I assume they are all alike. I guess this is how it works. But I hope I have sent inquiries to good, knowledgeable, reliable ones this time. I just need some decision making help from somebody who knows that they are talking about.

I don't trust you (yet). I don't know you, we've never met, so I can't trust you. Right now I have no clue who you are and if you are good at what you do. I read a little about you online and that is all. That is why I have asked for help from a couple of different agencies. If you respond to me quickly, read what I have written, and impress me all around, only then can I begin to trust you.

I am not happy being buried in your INBOX. A big fear is that you'll skip right over me. I do not know where my email to you goes. Are you sitting there eagerly awaiting my arrival, or do you check this once per week? I hope I am not buried there or you will delay my progress. I want to book a vacation and I need help now.

I am not junk mail. I am a real person. I travel every year, I have family, friends, and co-workers who travel. I did good research online about this vacation and even about you, before I sent my email. I am very real. I hope you are, too! I do not know if you are real or somebody sitting in a humongous call center with a fake name and a script. For all I know you are not even in the US! I am real and I need help from a pro.

I know you see me so please don't leave me. Faxes sometimes come through but emails always come through. I know you have a computer so I have arrived, no doubt. If you have a smart phone, my email arrived there, too. There is no valid excuse for you to miss me. The form I filled out online said nothing about you being out of the office, too busy for new leads, or uninterested in taking on new clients.

I want to have this conversation now! Yes, I am ready to finalize these vacation choices now. Today would be great, as I'm "in the vacation planning mode" right now. I want to take care of this before rates go up or availability dwindles or I get distracted. Help me now, please!

CHAPTER 4:

Why *your* INBOX?

I picked your INBOX because **someTHING sent mE**. It was not person. It was a thing like a website which had a CONTACT ME form. (If a person had referred mE, I probably would have called or at least mentioned their name.)

I liked what I saw. SomeTHING you wrote on the website appealed to me. Maybe it was your business name or description of your services. The photos may have helped. Bottom line, you offered mE help and I am here.

Actually, **I am here and there**. Because I don't know whether you will respond to mE or whether I will like you, I found another CONTACT ME form and asked them for help, too.

It's your move. Are you the one for mE? Once I clicked SEND, the ball moved to your court and the clock is ticking!

CHAPTER 5:
Which mE am I?

Every lead that appears is a potential client and friend.

Nobody completes CONTACT ME forms for *kicks*. No matter which mE I am, the moment I clicked SEND, I am in the game. I am exposed. Why on earth would I expose myself as a phony lead? Calling all TA's: Why are you so suspicious of mE? I have more at stake here. The TA who takes me seriously and proves to be a genuine professional will get my business.

I'd now like to introduce you to mE1, mE2, and mE3. You see, I come three ways and it is very important to know which has dropped in the box. You can determine which mE I am by reading what I have written to you (and perhaps between the lines):

mE1: "Just looking."
mE2: "Which is better?"
mE3: "Can you beat this?"

Knowing which mE I am is essential to our success. Know where my head is at before we talk. Read what I wrote on the CONTACT ME form. Each mE is at a different stage in the shopping process. That said, I assure you that each mE is ready to buy. The trick? Knowing how to deal with each type of mE.

Yes, we both want success!

Just as much as you want to make a sale, I want to book a vacation.

And since you have more than one client and I only have one vacation, I probably want this even more.

We're both on the same mission. In the next chapter I will tell you more about each mE so you'll know exactly how to help mE.

CHAPTER 6:

6 Critical Success Tips

1. It's about time. The first TA to touch mE has a better shot of winning the business—it's that simple. Timing is everything, even if I sent the inquiry to only one TA. Ideally, a personalized follow up should be same-day. If using an "auto-reply," which most companies send instantly to confirm receipt, then I expect instant confirmation!

2. Don't ask mE again. E filled out the inquiry form and sent it to you. Asking mE for the information already provided results in a big integrity-loss. I told you once and will not be too pleased having to say it twice.

3. I am ready to buy (yes, all 3 mE's). I took action to send you the lead. I am hot right now and want to complete the mission (to purchase the vacation). Even mE1 ("Just Looking") is prepared to purchase as quickly as mE3 (who is asking you to beat a price). *All mE's are in purchase mode now the moment they click SEND.*

4. I have relinquished control. Herein lies the TA's biggest opportunity—to recognize that I have passed you the ball. Yes, the ball is in your court. If you don't catch the ball and take control, you will lose it all. I would have never sent the inquiry otherwise. Consumers who don't wish to relinquish control never send inquiries in the first place. They never connect with TA's. They book online or directly with a supplier. So if a mE of any type does click SEND, take the reigns. Drive this bus!

5. I need validation. This might just be the single biggest nugget of advice. Apply this to all sales in order to win more and win big. Consumers who never send inquiries don't need outside validation, so they go direct or click "buy now." Everybody else (all e-inquiries like mE) will purchase once we receive validation in these four areas:

✓ *Validate that I have **chosen the right agent** for the job. Sell yourself and confirm you are a perfect fit for mE.*

✓ *Validate that I have **chosen the right product**. Whether I have already selected a product or you have guided mE expertly, make mE feel comfortable that this product is the best choice.*

✓ *Validate that I will be **paying the right price**. I want to hear you say that the price is right. I must feel good about the entire value-proposition. Tell mE it is excellent and squash any reason for mE to bother searching or price matching any further.*

✓ *Validate that **this is the right time to buy**. Clearly tell mE that this is the moment to wrap it up. Tell mE when the long journey of uncertainty has ended. Collecting payment signifies the end of shopping stress. It also marks the beginning of the new journey, which is the countdown to departure. I want to put this behind mE. It is a relief when we conclude a purchase, yes? Now I can do the paradigm shift: mark my calendar, tell friends, and start thinking of clothes to pack!*

6. There are three possible outcomes. Assuming you have successfully engaged mE, there are only three possible endings to this story:

o   If the TA does **really lousy work**: I book online (and never land in another TA's INBOX ever again). Basically, TA has successfully pushed mE over the line and into the universe of consumers who have lost all faith in travel agents.

o   If the TA does **generally lousy work**: I book with another TA—let's call that person INBOX2. We are assuming, of course, that INBOX2 did marginally better work!

o   If the TA does **excellent work:** I book with you! And if you really do a remarkably good job I won't be sending out inquiries any longer, nor searching the web for a travel agent to trust. I found you! Home at last.

CHAPTER 7:

Stop worrying about the ones that got away

"There are two people in this world. The ones you can help, and the ones you can't."

– Mike Marchev, master sales trainer

Attention TA: You can help mE but you can't help those who click BUY NOW. These people are either *savvy* or *ignorant*.

TA's can't help the *savvy* ones. They somehow figure it out (because they invest countless hours into research and analysis) and come home generally happy. Many brag about their decision-making independence. They are a proud group and consider themselves as skilled as you.

But I bet they would love to have that time back. Do you think they put a price tag on all the hours of investigation? Do you think they'll ever know about all the experiences missed because there was no TA involved? *That's why I am in your INBOX right now.*

As for folks in the *ignorant* category who are convinced that websites flat-out beat TA prices? You can't help them either. They are afraid of you. I am convinced they hold little regard and little respect for what you do for a living. I respect what you do. That's why I am in your INBOX right now.

Prove me right. Stop worrying about them and focus on mE. (Please know, however, that if you treat mE poorly, I might have no choice but to click BUY NOW.)

CHAPTER 8:

The psychology of mE3

"Can you beat this?"

Here are the secrets to making mE3 buy from you.

mE3 personality overview:

- **My business is out for bid.** But, there's more to me than just getting a cheaper price. *If I felt great about this purchase it would have already been done.* Tempting you for a price quote is how I choose to validate all of my choices. If you do give me a lower
price, I know you're more of a used-car salesman. If you just say no, that you can't beat it, and shut the door, then we'll never do business. Let's see how good you are at stopping mE in my tracks.

- **I am a second-class know-it-all.** If I were first-class, I would have booked online already without your help. I have done lots of research so I really do believe I know everything there is to know.

- **I am the toughest to engage.** This is why I asked one simple question. I am afraid to engage (though I will tell you the reason is that I don't have time).

- **I have little respect for TA's.** I have never met a TA that I liked…yet. Give me one good reason why I should like you. What makes you different than all the rest? My past experiences have been remarkably bad.

- **I am relationship-deprived.** Because every TA in my past blew mE off, I classify all TA's as order-takers. All you ever want is to make the sale. Whenever I have returned from my trip, you disappeared. *I wonder what it would be like to have a TA I could count on.* Going through this every year leaves me feeling used, abused, and low.

Want mE3 to buy from you? Here's what to do

- **Melt the ice/turn up the heat.** To get me to think of YOU as a person, warm up to mE. Prove to mE you are real, and that you really care about mE and my vacation.

- **Press pause.** I am focused on getting one thing from you, a better price. If you can distract me and slow mE down, you might get mE to down shift.

- **Change the target.** Turn my focus (aka target) away from price. Give me something else to think about. You need to get my attention and it had better be compelling.

- **Introduce fear.** Tell mE something I may have missed. What does my price not include? What surprise am I in for that the other TA (or online agency) has kept a secret? Shake mE up. Prove your worth to mE—validate your existence. What don't I know that will cost mE more in the long run? I want my vacation to be great, not cheap and just "ok."

- **Re-focus on your preferred brands.** If one of your brands is better than the one I have picked and you can prove it, I am all ears. Show mE you know more and you have my best interests in mind.

- **Supersize mE.** Perhaps you can pre-book certain things which may save mE money now and stress later. If you introduce mE to a better experience, I'll pay more to get a whole lot more. (It better be something that I need and may have missed when researching on my own.) Do a *needs assessment* before you offer. If I am unwilling to share, then dangle a long list of options in my face. I might spot something I really do need.

In summary:

Don't shudder when you see mE3 drop in the box! I am trying to intimidate you. Intimidate mE instead (gently and lovingly). Take mE on and win mE over.

CHAPTER 9:

The psychology of mE2

"Which is best?"

Here are the secrets to making mE2 buy from you.

mE2 personality overview:

- **I fear making the wrong choice.** I've gone far enough and now I am stuck. I cannot afford to blow this decision (or my family will be unforgiving!). I am willing to put the monkey on the back of a TA. I just hope you follow up quickly and know what you're talking about! I need your expertise, please.

- **I have done some homework.** I have done some research and made notes. That said, I can't spend any more time in front of my computer. Plus, I can't make heads or tails of all these blogs. Who to believe.

- **I am open for engagement.** I don't expect you to write back with one or the other as the best choice. I anticipate some back and forth. Please ask mE the right questions. That will impress mE. If you choose too quickly, or suggest another brand without knowing what is most important to mE, I will stop responding to your emails (or phone calls). Please make it about mE and not you.

- **I have a medium level of respect for TA's.** That's why I am here. My past experiences have been fairly unremarkable. I hope you are different.

- **I am empowering a TA (but not gifting you the sale).** I will be happy to have you book this for mE. Validate for me that you are the right agent, this is the right product, price, and time to buy.

Want mE2 to buy from you? Here's what to do

- **Understand my thinking.** Acknowledge my work. Recognize all the work I have done. Make mE feel good about the effort I already put in to this decision. Don't dismiss it or you risk insulting mE. Even if you differ with my analysis (and if you do, prove it!), at least compliment my research acumen and train of thought.

- **Establish your credibility.** Be confident in your recommendations. Tell me how you know so much. Do you have a certification? Have you been there yourself? Tell mE about your clients who loved their experience. Help mE to believe in you and the choices you suggest.

- **Confirm the target with you in it.** Take it over. Tell me that you've got everything under control from here. Be a part of the total experience. Remove the burden of making tough choices and tell mE everything's going to be OK. You've got my back. *When it is time to buy, I will be buying a stake in both you and the vacation.*

- **Focus on your preferred brands.** If you are a brand expert, that brings mE comfort. You can sway mE to your brand if you have great confidence (or promotional offers!).

In summary:

When mE2 drops in the box, get excited. I know what I want and I am eager. This sale is the TA's to lose. In other words, mE2 will buy somewhere else if this TA messes up. mE2 has simplified it and will have little patience if you don't answer their exact questions.

CHAPTER 10:

The psychology of mE1

"We're just looking."

Here are the secrets to making mE1 buy from you.

mE1 personality overview:

- **I am overwhelmed with choices.** Too many options for mE to digest. The Internet is overflowing with information. I just don't know what to believe and who to trust.

- **I am open to engage but afraid to lead a TA on.** I am not terribly comfortable coming to you, especially since I don't know exactly what I need. Please go easy on mE.

- **I believe purchase is far off.** Please don't think that I am ready to plunk down money right away. I would never buy something without feeling good about the product, the price and who I am buying from. Let's start at 50,000 feet and work from here. Let's see how it goes. Pushy selling tactics will drive mE away.

- **I've never had a great agent (but I do have faith).** I believe in TA's. I just haven't found one who is anything more than an order-taker. I would much prefer to have a go-to, trusted resource whenever a new vacation is on the horizon.

Want mE1 to buy from you? Here's what to do

- **Let mE "look" at my pace, no rushing!** I am secretly as ready to purchase as mE3 – I just don't know what to buy. Take it slow. Offer mE a cup of coffee and let mE look around. That translates to: Ask mE questions, present options. Let mE browse. When I see something I like, I will let you know.

- **Engage mE to qualify.** You know little about mE, so ask. I want to share. I am the most eager type of mE to accept your phone call. Make mE feel even better by requesting an appointment and setting a time limit for our call together.

- **I need hand holding.** I may be really skittish. Pay attention to any fears that surface while we chat. Recognize, legitimize, and assuage these fears and you may be in for years and years of vacation bookings.

- **I am actually ready to buy now.** I would not have exposed myself and entered the game unless I was ready to nail down my vacation plans. Don't be fooled by my "just looking" cover. *I said that to call off the dogs.*

- **I crave a relationship with a TA.** Spare mE from going through this year after year. Let's date, fall in love, and do business together for many years to come.

In summary:

Nobody buys without "just looking" first. Be grateful I did not look online and book there, too. Welcome mE to your store and let mE look all I want. Be happy I am here. Woo mE and I am yours!

CHAPTER 11:

How to connect with mE

Bummer! I am in your INBOX and not seated in your office. I am not even on the phone. I am in that vast, ever-expanding universe called INBOX, the great melting pot of personal, business, and senseless messages.

I arrive with no hand-shake, no eye contact, and no voice. If you were a detective, this would be your first big break in the case—the hot lead.

Leads turn cold quickly in law enforcement and in travel sales. Be a great detective. The difference? I want to be caught!

Our "engagement" objectives are quite different. I emailed you because I am uncomfortable calling you or giving you my phone number at this time. So, email mE first and maybe I will allow us a phone call later. Your objective is to get mE on the telephone so you can "sell" mE. I know you would prefer not to email back and forth either. However, that's as good as it's going to get right now—unless you are a remarkably good TA.

You will need to give mE a compelling reason to take your phone call.

I know that you will need to engage mE in order to sell mE—but also to obtain more information that is critical to planning this vacation.

The longer this process takes, the "colder" I get—sort of like a detective on a new case.

I will tell you a few tricks to engage mE. They are not really tricks as much as they are thoughtful strategies to convince mE to take your phone call.

Envision this process in three rounds…

Round 1: Impress mE quickly

If you send mE an "auto-reply" I will be pleased. That immediately confirms you received my e-inquiry. Want to make the experience better? Somehow personalize the text so it acknowledges that you know where the lead came from. Be sure to set my expectations so I know when I will hear from you next. Want the experience to be worse (and perhaps cost you the business)? Send me a generic auto-reply that has nothing to do with my inquiry.

If you choose not to send an "auto-reply" but email mE personally, I will be pleased and duly impressed. I realize this may sacrifice the speed at which you reply. However, your more personalized message will overcome that instantly. Be sure to set my expectations so I know when I will hear from you next.

Please remember that this first impression is critical to our relationship.

I will begin judging your expertise and likability instantly. Here's how to stand out from the INBOX2 reply:

a. **Begin telling mE your story.** Nothing too extensive, just enough of a picture so I get to know you (commonly known as your elevator speech or branding message).

b. **Get mE even more excited** about my vacation.

c. **Make mE feel welcomed.** I have entered your store. Create a welcoming environment so that I am comfortable.

d. **Express gratitude.** (You can never thank mE enough!)

Round 2: Engage

a. **Re-cap what I have already told you about my needs.** It's OK if you repeat it word for word. I may not have a copy of what I originally typed. This also confirms that you read what I wrote so we won't have to start over. Engage mE by making a comment or two about what I had written.

b. **Ask me a couple of questions** along the way. Simple ones. Best to give mE a choice. Therefore, I won't have to spend too much time typing my response. This makes it so much easier for mE. If I have the desire to write more, I will. However, a sprinkling of choice-type questions is all good and promotes healthy, safe engagement.

c. **Set expectations.** Please tell mE where we go from here. Tell mE what the next steps will be. That includes when I will hear back from you. Here, TA, is your chance to take control! If you don't take it, INBOX2 will.

Round 3: Connect

a. **Invite mE in for a 15-minute chat.** I like the fact that you put a time frame around a phone call. I feel safer committing. If our chat is going well, perhaps I will offer to extend our talk time. If not, I have permission to end our call after 15 minutes because that is your promise.

b. **Here are three fantastic questions** that will pique my interest and convince mE to connect by phone. Incorporate any or all of these into an email with mE:

1) **Tell mE you'd like to confirm things I don't want.** That will get my attention for sure. I may have a long list of things I should share so you know what I don't want to experience on this vacation. Glad you asked.

2) **Tell mE you'd like to suggest things I may want without realizing it.** Again you got my attention. I did some research so what could I have missed? Now you are striking up some fear that I may miss out—so good job getting my attention and convincing mE to connect.

3) **Tell mE you have found a promotion that I may qualify for.** I want great value here—so if you have an opportunity for mE to save money or get something special, I'm all ears.

TA, you've got one shot to engage and connect with me.

Since we have absolutely no relationship coming into this, it is just as easy for mE to walk away or just say "no thank you, not interested" if I am less than impressed from the get-go.

CHAPTER 12:

4 possible reasons why I am *not* returning your calls

And what if I don't reply to your initial emails—or any thereafter? Here are four possibilities:

1. Someone beat you to the punch.
2. I changed my mind.
3. I didn't like you.

All that said, there is a possible fourth reason I may have neglected you or been tardy with a reply:

4. Life got in the way!

So, don't lose all hope. There is a 25% chance I will be back. During this time period, be patient and courteous. I will be forever grateful if you give me time to focus on other issues I have at home or at work. Then, I will come back and be grateful you graciously waited for mE.

BONUS CHAPTER 13:

How to get mE to respond *faster*

How about 4 **bonus tips** to foster superior engagement?

1. Include your Facebook page, a photo of you, and/or a video link in your email.

2. Include a client testimonial—preferably, about something specific.

3. Include a slogan or "elevator speech" that really sums up what you're all about.

4. Tell mE if you have very specific recent experience or credentials relating to the vacation I am seeking.

BONUS
CHAPTER 14:
5 Don'ts

1. **Don't blame mE.** If I am contacting you about products you don't sell, don't blame mE. Something on your website or advertisement led mE to believe you did want this business. If the wrong inquires keep coming to you, you are sending the wrong message to the world.

   If you shout "deals and discounts" then your INBOX leads will be a special class of bargain hunter. If that's what you want, that's what you get.

2. **Don't delete mE.** If you delete mE, I will disappear from your INBOX. That solves one problem but creates another. You can be sure that I will tell my friends you never responded back to my e-lead.

3. **Don't desert mE.** If you start corresponding with mE, please don't slow or stop in the middle. I really don't care that a newer mE dropped in the box and that you got busy. I expect smooth, consistent, non-stop correspondence from you.

4. **Don't ask mE again.** If you ask "how can I help?" or "what can I help you with," I promise that you will not hear from mE again. At the very least you will have succeed in reducing my respect for you. Please don't ask mE to repeat what I already provided. If you do, then I know you failed to read my original submission (and *that* aggravates mE).

5. **Don't be the Office of Business Prevention.** When you answer the phone, it takes mE just a few seconds to feel welcomed, or not. Please don't answer the phone and give me the impression that I have just interrupted your day. On the contrary, make mE feel like I am the best call you have received all day. Make mE feel like you have been waiting for my call. You will either have mE at hello, or you'll lose mE. If you sound hurried or bothered, I will not be so eager to call back. Ever.

BONUS
CHAPTER 15:
11 Do's

1) **Do show mE you are real.** If your photo wasn't on the website or contact form, I have no clue who you are or what you look like. If I'm going to trust my vacation purchase to somebody, I'd very much like to "meet" you beyond just your email address. Please include a photo of you and as we begin to correspond, be personable. Let mE get to know you as a person, and not as a faceless, invisible entity that only exists inside my computer.

2) **Do tell mE where you are.** Are you in some vast call center or mammoth cubicle village halfway around the world? Or are you on Main Street USA sitting at a desk with pictures of your kids? Is your office at home? Tell mE where you. It will help mE visualize you better, trust you more, and strengthen our relationship.

3) **Do know where I came from.** I'll be terribly disappointed if you don't know where I came from. I assume you know where your CONTACT ME form resides. I assume you know where I came from when I plopped into your INBOX. To confirm this assumption, recognize that you already know this.

4) **Do establish credibility.** Prove to mE that you are a professional travel agent. Show mE how experienced you are (because it's not only about the number of years). Write like a pro, with no typos or abbreviations.

5) **Do begin validation.** I'll never admit that I need the four validations listed above, but I definitely do! Confirm that you are the right agent for mE, which is the right product for mE, what is the right price for mE, and that now is the best time to buy.

6) **Do give praise.** I put lots of thinking and research into my vacation so far. Earn a few brownie points by acknowledging the work I did. Make mE feel good that at least I'm on the right track. Plus, making me feel good about what I've done before will make me feel better about what I'm doing right now—consulting with you!

7) **Do express gratitude.** It is impossible to "over-thank" mE for being in your INBOX. Show mE how much you love mE and that you are excited to work with mE.

8) **Do demonstrate desire.** Do you desire my business? Do you desire to work with mE towards creating a fabulous trip? Let mE know in specific words.

9) **Do say my name.** Say my name! I am a real person. Talk to mE like you know mE.

10) **Do be authentic.** Be real. No need to put on a show and pretend to be someone you're not. I'd like to deal with the real "you." We might be friends if I like the real you! I'd rather not work with some flashy, fake, pompous sales person.

11) **Do say NO to mE.** If you disagree with my choices, just say no. If you don't wish to book this particular vacation choice, just say no. I'd much prefer that you tell mE so I can find an agent who fits my needs, choices, or personality better. Saying no saves us both lots of time. You can move on and so can I. Don't say yes to something you'll regret later!

Stuart's other resources will help you achieve higher levels of success and happiness!

Books:

Are You My Travel Agent? The 20 Step Plan For Putting Loyalty Back Into Your Business, by Stuart Lloyd Cohen

So you fear customer loyalty is dead? Travel agents felt an extraordinary competitive pinch from the Internet and a myriad of competitors. "Consumers don't stay loyal anymore", they cried. I strongly disagreed – which is why I wrote this powerful book demonstrating precisely how travel agents can still enjoy abundant client loyalty. Agents, get ready to experience a total transformation. I will convince you that consumers crave your loyalty even more. Loyalty will be alive and well for you starting today!

Available at: stuartlloydcohen.com/stuart-cohen-book-store

Video Courses:

YouTube channel: Stuart Lloyd Cohen

Talk show: stuartlloydcohen.com/stuart-cohen-show

Boot Camp by Stuart:

Sign-up: stuartlloydcohen.com/boot-camp-by-stuart

Never miss new blogs and get FREE motivational materials:

Twitter: @stuartcohenshow

Health & Wellness:

Free materials: healthysexyaging.com/follow-our-health-coach-blog

Twitter: @healthiersexier

Why do they call him *The Wrench*?

http://youtu.be/Qsl_WcA3720

NOTES:

www.ingramcontent.com/pod-product-compliance
Lightning Source LLC
Chambersburg PA
CBHW021852170526
45157CB00006B/2411